SUE BIRD: Queen of the Court

Tammy R. Julian

TABLE OF CONTENTS

SUE BIRD

INTRODUCTION

What does it take to be one of the greatest basketball players of all time? For Sue Bird, it started with a dream, a love for the game, and hours of practice on the court. From dribbling a ball as a little girl to leading her teams to championships, Sue's journey is nothing short of inspiring.

In this book, you'll discover how Sue went from being a kid with big dreams to a basketball legend. You'll learn about her challenges, her victories, and the lessons she shares with young athletes everywhere.

Whether you love basketball or simply want to hear the story of someone who worked hard to achieve greatness, Sue Bird's story will show you that anything is possible when you believe in yourself and give it your all.

Let's step onto the court and see how Sue became the Queen of the Court!

CHAPTER 1: WHO IS SUE BIRD

Sue Bird is one of the greatest basketball players of all time. Born on October 16, 1980, she is a retired professional basketball player known for her incredible skills as a point guard. She played for the Seattle Storm in the WNBA (Women's National Basketball Association) for 21 seasons, winning four WNBA championships.

Sue also represented the United States in five Olympic Games, winning gold medals every time, making her one of the most decorated athletes in basketball history. Known for her leadership, teamwork, and ability to make clutch plays, she became a role model for athletes worldwide.

Off the court, Sue is an advocate for equality, a mentor for young athletes, and a celebrated sports figure who inspires kids to chase their dreams.

A STAR IN THE MAKING

Sue Bird's basketball journey began in Syosset, New York, where she grew up in a family that loved sports. From the moment she picked up a basketball, Sue was hooked. She spent hours dribbling, shooting, and playing pick-up games in her driveway. Even as a young girl, her passion for the game was clear.

But it wasn't just passion that set Sue apart—it was her determination. In middle school, she joined local leagues and quickly stood out as one of the best players on the court. She wasn't the tallest or the strongest, but her quick thinking and sharp passes made her a natural leader.

In high school, Sue joined Christ the King Regional High School, one of the top basketball programs in New

York. There, she became a standout player. Her team won back-to-back state championships, and Sue's name began to spread in the basketball world. Scouts and coaches noticed her incredible ability to lead, score, and make her teammates better.

By the time she graduated, Sue was one of the most promising young players in the nation. But this was just the beginning. She knew the road ahead wouldn't be easy, but with her love for the game and her determination, Sue was ready to take her skills to the next level.

Sue Bird was on her way to becoming a basketball legend, one step at a time.

THE EARLY YEARS: SUE'S LOVE FOR THE GAME

Sue Bird's love for basketball started early. Growing up in Syosset, New York, she was always on the move, playing sports with her older sister, Jen, and friends in the neighborhood. But basketball was different—it felt like magic. She loved the sound of the ball bouncing on the pavement, the thrill of making a shot, and the teamwork that brought the game to life.

Sue's family noticed her talent and passion right away. Her dad often played basketball with her, encouraging her to practice dribbling, passing, and shooting. Even as a young girl, Sue showed incredible focus and determination. She didn't just play for fun; she wanted to get better every day.

Her competitive spirit grew stronger when she started playing in local youth leagues. Sue wasn't the tallest player on the court, but her speed, smart plays, and incredible court vision made her stand out. She quickly became a key player, impressing coaches and teammates alike.

Basketball wasn't just a game for Sue—it was a dream. Those early years laid the foundation for her journey to becoming one of the greatest players of all time.

HIGH SCHOOL DREAMS: BECOMING A LEADER

When Sue Bird joined Christ the King Regional High School in Queens, New York, she stepped onto one of the most competitive basketball stages in the country. Known for its powerhouse basketball program, the school pushed Sue to sharpen her skills and rise to a whole new level. It didn't take long for her to shine.

As a freshman, Sue's quick passes, smooth shots, and smart plays made her a standout player. But she could bring her team together which truly set her apart. She wasn't just playing for herself—she wanted everyone on her team to succeed. Her leadership on the court inspired her teammates and caught the attention of coaches and fans.

In her junior and senior years, Sue led her team to back-to-back state championships. Her poise under pressure and knack for making game-changing plays earned her recognition as one of the best high school players in the country. Scouts from top colleges were lining up to recruit her, and her dream of playing basketball at the highest level was becoming a reality.

High school was where Sue Bird truly began to shine as a leader. It was clear that she wasn't just a great player—she was destined to become a legend.

CHAPTER 2: COLLEGE CHAMPION

Sue Bird's journey to greatness continued when she joined the University of Connecticut (UConn), one of the most successful women's basketball programs in the country. Playing under legendary coach Geno Auriemma, Sue quickly learned what it took to compete at the highest level.

Her freshman year was challenging as she adjusted to the speed and skill of college basketball, but Sue's determination and work ethic helped her rise to the occasion. By her sophomore year, she was the starting point guard, leading her team with precision passing, smart decision-making, and a calmness that inspired her teammates.

In 2002, Sue's senior year, she helped lead UConn to an unforgettable season. The team went undefeated, winning all 39 games and earning the NCAA Championship. Sue's leadership on and off the court was a key factor in their success. She was named the National Player of the Year and earned the prestigious Nancy Lieberman Award for being the best point guard in the nation.

During her time at UConn, Sue Bird became more than just a great player—she became a champion. Her ability to lead, perform under pressure, and make her teammates better solidified her legacy as one of the greatest players in college basketball history.

UCONN SUCCESS: A DYNASTY BEGINS

When Sue Bird stepped onto the University of Connecticut (UConn) campus, she didn't just join a team—she became part of a basketball dynasty in the making. UConn women's basketball was already one of the best programs in the country, and under the guidance of legendary coach Geno Auriemma, Sue had the perfect environment to grow into the player she was meant to be.

From her very first game, it was clear that Sue was a special talent. As the starting point guard, she took charge of the court, running plays, setting up her teammates, and making smart, calculated decisions under pressure. Her ability to control the game and her sharp basketball IQ quickly earned her the respect of coaches, teammates, and fans alike.

In her freshman year, UConn made it to the NCAA Tournament, but it wasn't until Sue's sophomore year that the team started to hit their stride. Alongside her teammates, including future WNBA stars, Sue led UConn to multiple Final Fours and national titles. Their dominance was undeniable.

By her senior year, Sue had helped the UConn Huskies win the NCAA Championship in 2002, finishing with an undefeated season. Her leadership, poise, and clutch performances made her one of the most successful and celebrated college athletes of all time.

Sue Bird wasn't just a part of the UConn dynasty—she helped build it. Her time at UConn solidified the program's place as one of the greatest in college basketball history, and she laid the foundation for future generations of athletes to follow.

WINNING IT ALL: SUE'S FIRST BIG TITLE

Sue Bird's college career reached its pinnacle in 2002 when she and her UConn teammates achieved something extraordinary—an undefeated season and the NCAA Championship. After years of hard work, practice, and teamwork, Sue finally reached the top of the mountain.

The road to the championship wasn't easy. UConn faced tough competition throughout the season, but Sue's leadership on the court made all the difference. As the point guard, she ran the offense smoothly, making key passes and helping her teammates shine. Her ability to stay calm under pressure, especially in close games, was crucial to the team's success.

In the championship game, Sue played a critical role, contributing points, assists, and key defensive plays. Her poise and confidence lifted the entire team, and when the final buzzer sounded, UConn had secured a perfect 39-0 record and their second national title in four years.

Winning it all was a moment Sue would never forget. It was the first major title of her career, and it showed the world what she was capable of. Her performance earned her the prestigious NCAA Tournament Most Outstanding Player award, and she had officially cemented herself as one of the best in the game.

That championship title wasn't just a personal victory—it was the beginning of Sue Bird's legacy as a winner and a leader, setting the stage for even more championships and successes to come.

SUE BIRD

The 2002 NCAA Championship wasn't just a victory for Sue Bird—it was the beginning of her legacy as a clutch performer. Her leadership and vision on the court made her a standout player in that title game, but she could make her teammates better which truly set her apart. Sue didn't just focus on scoring points; she focused on running the offense, creating opportunities for others, and setting up plays that led to victory.

Throughout the tournament, Sue showcased her versatility as a point guard. She controlled the pace of the game, calmed her teammates when they needed it most and made critical assists at the right moments. In the final game, her smart decisions and composed play under pressure helped UConn overcome their opponent, proving that her ability to lead wasn't just about talent—it was about trust, teamwork, and confidence in her role as a playmaker.

After the championship win, Sue Bird was celebrated as one of the best players in college basketball, earning numerous accolades, including the NCAA Tournament's

Most Outstanding Player Award. She had reached the peak of college basketball and left an unforgettable mark on the UConn program.

But Sue knew this victory was just the beginning of a much bigger journey. She had tasted success at the collegiate level, and now it was time to set her sights on the WNBA and the professional stage, where even greater challenges and opportunities awaited. Winning the NCAA Championship wasn't just about earning a trophy—it was about proving to herself

f and the world that she could succeed at the highest level, and she was ready to take on whatever came next.

CHAPTER 3: RISING IN THE WNBA

After a legendary college career, Sue Bird was ready to take on the professional world. In 2002, she was selected as the first overall pick in the WNBA Draft by the Seattle Storm, marking the beginning of her long and successful career in the league.

At first, Sue faced the challenge of adjusting to the faster and more physical game of the WNBA, but her experience at UConn had prepared her well. She quickly proved herself as a smart, skilled point guard, using her incredible vision on the court to set up her teammates and lead the offense. In her very first season, she made an immediate impact, earning the WNBA Rookie of the Year award.

Sue's ability to run the floor, make pinpoint passes, and stay calm under pressure made her a perfect fit for the Seattle Storm. Over the years, she built a strong partnership with her teammates, especially with star players like Lauren Jackson. Together, they formed a dynamic duo that would lead the Storm to great success.

By 2004, Sue's hard work and leadership paid off when she helped the Seattle Storm win their first-ever WNBA Championship. It was a huge milestone in her career, and Sue's ability to perform in big moments showed that she was more than just a rising star—she was a winner.

Sue's journey in the WNBA had only just begun, but with her natural talent, leadership skills, and determination, it was clear that she was destined for greatness. As she continued to rise in the league, Sue Bird became known not just as one of the best point guards in the WNBA, but as one of the most respected players in women's basketball history.

DRAFT DAY: JOINING THE SEATTLE STORM

Sue Bird's dream of playing professional basketball became a reality on April 30, 2002, when she was selected as the first overall pick in the WNBA Draft by the Seattle Storm. It was a moment she had worked for her entire life, and it marked the beginning of her legendary career in the league.

Draft day was filled with excitement and nerves as Sue sat with her family and friends, waiting to hear her name called. When it finally happened, the excitement was overwhelming. Sue was heading to Seattle—a city known for its passionate sports fans and a team with big aspirations. She was ready to take on the challenge and prove she belonged among the best.

Joining the Seattle Storm was the perfect fit for Sue. From the very beginning, she felt at home in the team's system. With her incredible basketball IQ and leadership qualities, Sue quickly earned the trust of her coaches and teammates. She wasn't just focused on scoring; she was determined to make everyone around her better, using her playmaking skills to set up teammates for easy shots.

In her first season with the Storm, Sue quickly made her mark, earning the WNBA Rookie of the Year award. Her passing, court vision, and ability to control the game were unmatched, and it became clear that she was going to be a force in the league for years to come. The Storm had found their leader, and Sue Bird's professional career was off to an incredible start.

Draft day was just the beginning of what would become a storied career in Seattle, one that would include multiple championships, countless records, and a lasting legacy as one of the greatest point guards in WNBA history.

A CAREER OF CHAMPIONSHIPS

From the moment Sue Bird joined the Seattle Storm, she set her sights on one goal: winning championships. Over the years, her dedication, leadership, and skill would turn that dream into a reality, making her one of the most successful players in WNBA history.

Sue's first championship came in 2004 when the Seattle Storm claimed their very first WNBA title. In that series, Sue showcased her ability to perform under pressure, running the offense and making crucial plays at key moments. Her leadership helped guide the Storm to a 2-1 victory over the Connecticut Sun, and Sue earned her first championship ring. It was a sweet moment for Sue, but it also ignited her desire to win even more titles.

Over the next several years, Sue continued to be the heart and soul of the Storm. She was known for her consistency, poise, and ability to elevate her game when it mattered most. In 2010, the Storm clinched another WNBA title, with Sue once again playing a pivotal role in their success. Her ability to control the flow of the game, create opportunities for her teammates, and make key shots in crunch time made her a standout in the playoffs.

Sue's championship success wasn't just about individual talent; it was about teamwork. She formed strong bonds with her teammates, including stars like Lauren Jackson and Breanna Stewart, and together they built one of the most dominant teams in the league. Sue's leadership on and off the court inspired her teammates to reach new heights, and the Storm won their third championship in 2018.

With four WNBA titles to her name, Sue Bird had cemented herself as one of the most decorated players in the history of the league. Each championship she earned was a testament to her hard work, dedication, and love for the game. Sue's career wasn't just about winning titles—it was about creating a legacy of excellence, inspiring future generations of players, and proving that with the right mindset, anything is possible.

As Sue Bird's career continued, her drive to win championships remained as strong as ever. Even as the years went by, her leadership and ability to elevate her game never wavered. Her influence extended beyond her performances—she became a key mentor to younger players, teaching them the importance of teamwork, hard work, and resilience.

In 2018, Sue and the Seattle Storm reached the pinnacle of success once again. With a perfect blend of veteran leadership and fresh talent, they won their third WNBA Championship. Sue's steady presence on the court, her incredible playmaking, and her unshakable focus in the playoffs were crucial to their victory. She led by example, showing her teammates the heart and determination needed to succeed. The Storm's triumph was a full-circle moment for Sue, as she had helped build this championship team from the ground up, much like she had done in 2004.

Sue's success wasn't just limited to the WNBA. She also played a crucial role in helping Team USA secure multiple Olympic gold medals, including in 2004, 2008, 2012, 2016, and 2020. Her international achievements only added to her legacy, proving that Sue Bird's impact extended far beyond the WNBA. She became one of the most decorated athletes in basketball history, showing that with perseverance, leadership, and a love for the game, success is possible on any stage.

By the end of her career, Sue had solidified her place as one of the best point guards ever to play the game. Four WNBA championships, five Olympic gold medals, and countless accolades proved that Sue Bird was more than just a star—she was a true legend.

Her career was not just about the titles she won, but the way she led and inspired others along the way. Through every victory and challenge, Sue's legacy was built on her dedication to the game, her love for her teammates, and her unwavering belief in the power of hard work and teamwork. As she retired from the WNBA in 2022, Sue Bird left behind a legacy that would inspire athletes for generations to come.

CHAPTER 4: ON THE WORLD STAGE

Sue Bird's incredible talent and leadership weren't confined to the WNBA. She also made a significant impact on the global stage, representing the United States in international competitions and helping Team USA dominate women's basketball for nearly two decades.

Sue first made her mark on the world stage at the 2004 Olympic Games in Athens, where she helped lead Team USA to a gold medal. From that moment on, she became a mainstay on the U.S. women's basketball team, earning a reputation as one of the best point guards in the world. Her basketball IQ, ability to control the tempo of the game, and knack for making clutch plays made her an invaluable asset to Team USA.

Over the years, Sue continued to help Team USA achieve success, winning gold medals in every Olympic Games she competed in 2004, 2008, 2012, 2016, and

2020. Her leadership, both on and off the court, was crucial to the team's success. Sue played a key role in bringing together players from different backgrounds and making sure everyone understood the importance of teamwork and sacrifice. She taught her teammates that winning wasn't just about individual talent—it was about playing for the team and supporting each other to achieve the ultimate goal.

Sue's success on the world stage wasn't limited to the Olympics. She also competed in FIBA World Cup tournaments, where she continued to help Team USA win gold. Her performances on the international stage made her one of the most decorated and respected athletes in the world, and her achievements with Team USA further cemented her status as a basketball legend.

Representing her country and competing against the best players in the world was a source of great pride for Sue. She was not just playing for herself or her team; she was playing for her country, and each gold medal she earned was a testament to her hard work, dedication, and passion for the game.

Sue Bird's success on the world stage helped elevate women's basketball globally, inspiring young athletes everywhere to dream big and work hard to achieve greatness. Her legacy as a leader and a champion extends far beyond the WNBA, and she will always be remembered as one of the most accomplished basketball players in history.

TEAM USA: CHASING OLYMPIC GOLD

Sue Bird's journey with Team USA began in 2004 when she made her Olympic debut in Athens. That year, she helped lead the U.S. women's basketball team to a gold medal, starting a streak that would last for nearly two decades. Sue's leadership, playmaking, and poise under pressure became key ingredients in Team USA's success, and she quickly became one of the most respected players on the team.

In the years that followed, Sue continued to chase the dream of Olympic gold. Each Olympic Games presented new challenges, but Sue's unwavering dedication to the team and her leadership on the court helped Team USA maintain its dominance. Her ability to set up teammates, control the flow of the game, and perform in clutch moments made her a vital part of the team's success.

In 2008, 2012, and 2016, Sue Bird was there, helping guide Team USA to victory, and each time, she cemented her legacy as one of the greatest international basketball players in history. The Olympic gold medals kept coming, and Sue became known as a leader who could inspire and elevate her teammates, no matter the stage.

By the time the 2020 Tokyo Olympics came around, Sue was one of the most experienced players on the team, but her hunger for another gold medal was just as strong as ever. Despite facing stiff competition from other nations, Team USA, with Sue's leadership, won their seventh consecutive gold medal in women's basketball. Sue had played in five Olympic Games, earning five gold medals, and cementing her place as one of the greatest to ever play the game.

For Sue Bird, chasing Olympic gold was about more than just winning. It was about the pride of representing her country and inspiring future generations of athletes. Throughout her career, Sue showed that leadership, dedication, and teamwork are the keys to achieving greatness, and her Olympic success will forever be a part of her lasting legacy.

INSPIRING THE WORLD: SUE'S GLOBAL IMPACT

Sue Bird's impact extended far beyond the basketball court. Her achievements in the WNBA and on the international stage have inspired millions of young athletes, especially girls, to pursue their dreams and believe in the power of hard work and dedication. Throughout her career, Sue showed the world that talent, passion, and leadership can break barriers and change lives.

As one of the most successful and respected players in women's basketball, Sue used her platform to advocate for equality, women's sports, and the next generation of athletes. She was vocal about the importance of creating opportunities for women in sports, both on and off the court. Sue worked to ensure that female athletes received the same recognition, respect, and opportunities as their male counterparts, helping to inspire a movement of change in the world of sports.

Sue's influence reached far beyond the United States. Her success with Team USA and her international accomplishments in the WNBA inspired countless young athletes around the world. Whether they were in Asia, Europe, or Africa, girls and boys alike looked up to Sue as a role model, not just for her basketball skills but for her leadership, integrity, and commitment to making the world a better place through sport.

In addition to her basketball achievements, Sue's advocacy for social justice and her commitment to making a difference in her community and the world have solidified her legacy as a true champion, both on and off the court. She showed young athletes everywhere that it's not just about the games you win, but how you use your success to lift others and inspire change.

Sue Bird's global impact is felt not just in the basketball world but in communities around the globe. Through her career, she proved that one person—through determination, leadership, and a commitment to making a difference—can inspire millions and change the world.

Sue Bird's influence stretched far beyond her on-court accomplishments. Her role as an ambassador for women's sports has inspired a global movement that's empowering young athletes, particularly girls, to break through barriers. By being unapologetically herself—confident, passionate, and driven—Sue has shown that women can excel in sports and leadership roles, encouraging young people everywhere to chase their dreams without limits.

Throughout her career, Sue didn't just focus on basketball—she used her voice to speak out for equality and inclusion. She became a vocal advocate for LGBTQ+ rights and social justice, speaking candidly about the need for equality in sports and beyond. Sue demonstrated that athletes have the power to make a difference in the world by standing up for what is right, and she paved the way for future athletes to use their platforms for positive change.

Sue's impact was also evident in how she mentored the next generation of players. As a leader on Team USA, she played a crucial role in guiding younger players and sharing her wisdom and experience. Sue was always willing to help her teammates grow, whether it was on the court, offering advice, or off the court, encouraging them to become leaders themselves.

Internationally, Sue's basketball achievements inspired children everywhere. Her success in the Olympics, WNBA, and Team USA showed kids that with hard work, focus, and perseverance, anything is possible. Sue Bird became more than just a basketball legend—she became a beacon of hope and possibility for athletes of all backgrounds around the world.

Sue's global impact is a reminder that greatness is about more than just individual success. It's about using your platform to inspire change, lifting others as you rise, and believing that together, we can create a better world. Sue Bird's legacy is one of courage, empowerment, and, most importantly, love for the game and its ability to unite and inspire people across the globe.

CHAPTER 5: LESSONS FROM SUE BIRD

Sue Bird’s remarkable career offers countless lessons that go far beyond basketball. Her journey is filled with examples of hard work, leadership, resilience, and the power of staying true to oneself. Here are some key lessons that young athletes—and anyone striving to be their best—can take from Sue Bird’s life and career:

1. Leadership is About Teamwork

Sue Bird's greatest strength wasn't just her skill—it was her ability to make those around her better. She showed that great leaders empower others. Whether on the court or in life, true leadership is about guiding, supporting, and inspiring those around you to reach their potential.

2. Never Stop Growing

Sue's success wasn't built on talent alone. She was always learning, always working to improve, and never settling for "good enough." Whether it was adapting to the speed of the WNBA or facing new challenges with Team USA, Sue demonstrated that growth never stops. To succeed, you must be willing to constantly evolve and push yourself beyond your limits.

3. Overcome Challenges with Positivity

Throughout her career, Sue faced setbacks—injuries, tough losses, and moments of doubt. But she always bounced back with a positive attitude. Sue's resilience taught us that challenges aren't roadblocks; they are opportunities to grow stronger and more determined. The key is staying positive and focused on your goals.

4. Play with Purpose

Sue played not just for herself, but for something bigger. Every game was an opportunity to represent her country, her team, and the next generation of athletes. She showed that playing with purpose—whether in sports, school, or life—gives you the motivation to give your best and make a difference in the world.

5. Believe in Yourself

Sue Bird had an unwavering belief in her abilities, even when others doubted her. She wasn't always the tallest or the fastest, but she knew her strengths and trusted in them. Her journey teaches us that confidence and self-belief are key to overcoming obstacles and achieving greatness.

6. Be a Role Model

Beyond basketball, Sue Bird's work as an advocate for equality and social justice shows the importance of using your platform for good. Whether in sports or any field, being a role model means doing the right thing, standing up for others, and inspiring people to follow in your footsteps.

7. Success Comes with Sacrifice

Sue Bird didn't achieve her success without making sacrifices—time away from family, countless hours of practice, and a commitment to her team. She taught us that success doesn't come easy; it requires dedication, discipline, and the willingness to make sacrifices for the greater good.

8. Never Give Up on Your Dreams

Sue's story is one of perseverance. From her early years in basketball to her rise as a WNBA and Olympic champion, Sue never gave up on her dreams. She showed us that no dream is too big if you're willing to work for it and believe in it, even when the road seems difficult.

Sue Bird's lessons resonate far beyond the basketball court. Her life reminds us that greatness isn't just about winning—it's about hard work, leadership, resilience, and lifting others as you rise. Through her actions, Sue has taught us how to be better athletes, better leaders, and better people.

HARD WORK AND TEAMWORK

Sue Bird's career is a shining example of how hard work and teamwork are the keys to success, both in basketball and in life. From her early years in the sport to her legendary WNBA career, Sue always prioritized both her effort and her role within a team, understanding that great achievements are rarely accomplished alone.

1. The Power of Hard Work

Sue Bird's talent was undeniable, but her success didn't come from natural ability alone. She spent countless hours honing her skills—practicing her passing, improving her defense, and refining her basketball IQ. Hard work was the foundation of her success. Sue's relentless drive to get better each day is a powerful lesson: talent may open the door, but hard work is what keeps you in the game.

Whether it was preparing for the Olympics or training for a crucial WNBA season, Sue never took shortcuts.

Her work ethic pushed her beyond what seemed possible, setting a standard for excellence that inspired those around her. Sue showed that when you put in the effort, you can achieve things that others might think are out of reach.

2. Teamwork Makes the Dream Work

While Sue's skills made her one of the best players in the world, she knew that basketball is a team sport, and no one can win alone. Throughout her career, Sue always focused on the importance of teamwork, whether it was with her Seattle Storm teammates or with Team USA. She understood that everyone has a role to play, and success comes from working together toward a common goal.

On the court, Sue made sure to set up her teammates for success, whether by dishing out assists, creating opportunities, or encouraging them when times got tough. Her leadership wasn't just about scoring points—it was about making the team better as a whole. Sue showed that when every member of a team is committed to working together, there are no limits to what can be achieved.

Beyond basketball, Sue's emphasis on teamwork also extends to the importance of supporting one another in everyday life. She worked hard to build relationships with her teammates and foster a sense of unity and trust. In doing so, Sue created an environment where everyone felt valued and supported, and in return, the team achieved great success.

The Takeaway

Sue Bird's approach to hard work and teamwork is a reminder that success is not just about individual achievements—it's about the effort you put in and the way you work with others to reach your goals. Her dedication and focus on making the team better inspired everyone around her, proving that the greatest victories are those earned together. Whether you're on the basketball court, in the classroom, or at work, Sue Bird's example teaches us that with hard work and strong teamwork, anything is possible.

DREAM BIG, PLAY BIG: ADVICE FOR YOUNG ATHLETES

Sue Bird's journey from a young basketball player to a WNBA legend is a testament to the power of dreaming big and playing big. Throughout her career, she has always encouraged young athletes to believe in themselves, push beyond their limits, and embrace the hard work required to achieve their dreams. Here's some of the best advice Sue has for young athletes who aspire to greatness:

1. Believe in Yourself

Sue Bird's path to success wasn't always easy, and she faced plenty of doubters along the way. But one thing she always had was confidence in her abilities. Her advice to young athletes is simple: "Believe in yourself, even when others might not." Confidence is the first step toward achieving your goals. When you trust in your abilities, you can tackle challenges head-on and keep pushing toward your dreams.

2. Dream Big

Sue always dreamed of playing professional basketball, and she never let anything stand in her way. Her message to young athletes is to aim high and dream big—don't limit yourself by what others say is possible. Dreaming big opens up a world of possibilities and gives you something to work toward, no matter how difficult the journey may seem. Sue shows us that when you have a big dream and work relentlessly toward it, amazing things can happen.

3. Embrace the Journey, Not Just the Destination

While winning championships and Olympic gold medals are incredible achievements, Sue Bird teaches that the real joy comes from the journey. It's about growing as an athlete, learning from failures, and building relationships with teammates. Young athletes should focus on enjoying the process of improving and having fun along the way. Success comes when you put in the work, but the memories and experiences from the journey are what truly shape you.

4. Work Hard Every Day

Sue Bird's success didn't happen overnight. It came from years of hard work, dedication, and sacrifice. Her advice to young athletes is to put in the effort every day, whether it's in practice, school, or life. Hard work is the key to turning dreams into reality. Every time you practice, you get one step closer to your goal, and the more effort you put in, the better you'll become.

5. Learn from Setbacks

No athlete's journey is without setbacks. Sue faced injuries, tough losses, and moments where things didn't go as planned. But she always bounced back, learning from those challenges. Sue teaches that setbacks are a natural part of growth and should be seen as opportunities to learn and improve. When things don't go your way, don't give up—use it as fuel to come back stronger.

6. Be a Team Player

While individual skills are important, Sue Bird knows that basketball (and most sports) is about the team. She was always focused on making those around her better, whether by passing the ball, motivating teammates, or offering guidance. Being a great teammate is just as important as being a great player. Sue's advice is to always support your teammates, because working together as a team is what leads to success.

7. Stay True to Who You Are

Throughout her career, Sue stayed true to herself. She always played with authenticity and passion, never trying to be someone she wasn't. Her advice to young athletes is to embrace their uniqueness and play in a way that reflects who they are. The best athletes are the ones who stay true to their values, work hard, and trust their instincts.

The Takeaway

Sue Bird's story is one of perseverance, hard work, and never giving up on your dreams. For young athletes looking to follow in her footsteps, her advice is clear:

Dream big, work hard every day, embrace the journey, and always be a team player. Most importantly, believe in yourself and trust that with determination, anything is possible. By playing big and dreaming big, you can achieve great things—just like Sue Bird did.

CONCLUSION

Sue Bird's journey from a young basketball enthusiast to one of the greatest players in the world is an inspiring story of hard work, dedication, and leadership. Through her incredible career in the WNBA, her Olympic gold medal victories, and her advocacy for equality, Sue showed the world what it truly means to dream big and work tirelessly to achieve those dreams.

Her legacy is not just in the championships and records she set but in the way she lifted others, empowered her teammates, and used her platform to create positive change. Sue Bird has proven that greatness is not only about winning—it's about inspiring others to do their best, no matter the challenges.

For young athletes everywhere, Sue's story serves as a reminder that with passion, determination, and a commitment to both personal growth and teamwork, anything is possible. Sue Bird didn't just play the game; she changed it, and her influence will continue to inspire future generations for years to come.

FUN FACTS

1. A Multi-Sport Star

Before focusing solely on basketball, Sue Bird was a talented athlete in other sports, including soccer and tennis. She was a natural athlete, excelling in whatever she tried!

2. Olympic Gold Medals

Sue Bird has won five Olympic gold medals with Team USA in women's basketball—one in each of the 2004, 2008, 2012, 2016, and 2020 Olympic Games. She's one of the most decorated female athletes in Olympic history.

3. A Record-Setting Career

Sue Bird holds the record for the most assists in WNBA history, showcasing her incredible court vision and playmaking abilities. She truly made her teammates better!

4. A Basketball Family

Sue's father, Herschel Bird, was a basketball player in college, and her brother, also named Herschel, played college basketball too. It seems basketball talent runs in the family!

5. Basketball at UConn

Sue Bird played college basketball at the University of Connecticut (UConn), where she led her team to two NCAA championships. Her time there helped her become one of the best college basketball players in history.

6. A Love for Fashion

Outside of basketball, Sue has an interest in fashion. She's known for her stylish wardrobe and has even made appearances at fashion events, showing that she has a creative side off the court too!

7. Incredible Longevity

Sue Bird played for the Seattle Storm for her entire 19-year WNBA career, making her one of the longest-serving athletes in the league. Her commitment to one team is something very rare in professional sports.

8. An Advocate for Equality

Sue Bird is a passionate advocate for gender equality in sports and social justice issues. She’s used her platform to speak out about important causes, showing that athletes can make a difference in the world beyond their sport.

9. A True Winner

Sue Bird has won a WNBA championship four times with the Seattle Storm, proving her incredible skill and leadership on the court. She's one of the greatest point guards the WNBA has ever seen.

10. Retirement Announcement in 2022

After an outstanding career, Sue Bird officially announced that the 2022 season would be her final year.

It was a bittersweet moment for fans, but her legacy lives on in the basketball world forever.

QUIZ

Test your knowledge of the legendary Sue Bird! Answer the following questions to see how much you know about her amazing career and life.

1. Where did Sue Bird play college basketball?
   a) Stanford University
   b) University of Connecticut (UConn)
   c) Duke University
   d) University of Texas

2. How many Olympic gold medals has Sue Bird won?
   a) 3
   b) 4
   c) 5
   d) 6

3. What team did Sue Bird play for throughout her entire WNBA career?

a) New York Liberty
b) Los Angeles Sparks
c) Seattle Storm
d) Chicago Sky

4. In which year did Sue Bird make her Olympic debut?

a) 2000
b) 2004
c) 2008
d) 2012

5. How many WNBA championships has Sue Bird won with the Seattle Storm?

a) 2
b) 3
c) 4
d) 5

6. Which record does Sue Bird hold in the WNBA?

a) Most career points
b) Most career assists
c) Most three-pointers made
d) Most rebounds in a single game

7. Sue Bird is known for advocating for which of the following causes?

a) Animal rights
b) Gender equality in sports
c) Climate change
d) Space exploration

8. What other sport did Sue Bird excel in before focusing on basketball?

a) Soccer
b) Tennis
c) Swimming
d) Baseball

9. Sue Bird is considered one of the greatest point guards in WNBA history. What is one of her best-known skills on the court?

a) Scoring

b) Rebounding

c) Assists and playmaking

d) Blocking shots

10. When did Sue Bird announce that the 2022 season would be her final season in the WNBA?

a) 2019

b) 2020

c) 2021

d) 2022

ANSWER KEY:

1. b) University of Connecticut (UConn)
2. c) 5
3. c) Seattle Storm
4. b) 2004
5. c) 4
6. b) Most career assists
7. b) Gender equality in sports

8. a) Soccer

9. c) Assists and playmaking

10. d) 2022

Made in the USA
Columbia, SC
11 December 2024

49002169R00033